W9-COD-615

How's the Weather?

A Look at Weather and How It Changes

By Melvin and Gilda Berger
Illustrated by John Emil Cymerman

Property of:
Edison Kenwood Charter School

Ideals Children's Books • Nashville, Tennessee

The authors, artist, and publisher wish to thank the following for their invaluable advice and instruction for this book:

Jane Hyman, B.S., M.Ed. (Reading), M.Ed. (Special Needs), C.A.E.S. (Curriculum, Administration, and Supervision)

Rose Feinberg, B.S., M.Ed. (Elementary Education), Ed.D. (Reading and Language Arts)

R.L. 2.1 Spache

Text copyright © 1993 by Melvin and Gilda Berger
Illustrations copyright © 1993 by John Emil Cymerman

All rights reserved. No part of this publication may be reproduced or transmitted in any form or by any means, electronic or mechanical, including photocopy, recording, or any information storage and retrieval system, without permission in writing from the publisher.

Published by Ideals Children's Books
An imprint of Hambleton-Hill Publishing, Inc.
Nashville, Tennessee 37218

Printed and bound in Mexico

Library of Congress Cataloging-in-Publication Data

Berger, Melvin.
    How's the weather? : a look at weather and how it changes / by
Melvin and Gilda Berger ; illustrated by John Emil Cymerman.
        p.   cm.—(Discovery readers)
    Includes index.
    Summary: Discusses how and why the weather changes and ways
to predict the weather by observing the sky, clouds, and wind.
        ISBN 0-8249-8641-5 (lib. bdg.)—ISBN 0-8249-8599-0 (pbk.)
    1. Weather—Juvenile literature. 2. Meteorology—Juvenile literature.
[1. Weather. 2. Meteorology.] I. Berger, Gilda. II. Cymerman, John Emil,
ill. III. Title. IV. Series.
QC981.3.B47   1993
551.5—dc20   93-16686
                                                                            CIP
                                                                            AC

How's the Weather? is part of the *Discovery Readers*® series.
Discovery Readers is a registered trademark of Hambleton-Hill Publishing,

How's the weather?
Look at the sky.

The sun is shining.
There are few clouds.
The day is warm and sunny.

3

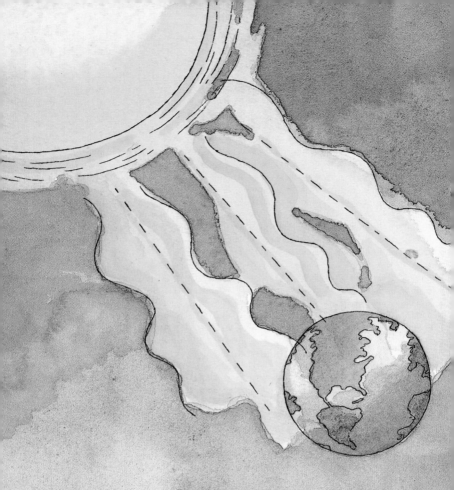

The sun is like a giant lamp in space.
It gives off rays of light and heat.
The sun's rays travel a long way to
 Earth.
Its light rays light the earth.
Its heat rays warm the earth.

We see shadows on sunny days.
Shadows form when things block the
  sun's light.
Trees, buildings, you, and I—
  we all make shadows.

During the day the sun moves across
the sky.
This makes shadows change.
They move from one side of objects to
the other.
A sundial was one of the first clocks.
It uses the moving shadow cast by the
sun to tell time.

It's fun to play outdoors on sunny days.
But the sun's rays are bad for your
skin.
Too much sun can cause a bad sunburn.
It can cause spots and wrinkles to form
on your skin when you get older.
Cover up with sunscreen!

How's the weather?
Look at the sky.

The sky is gray.
Clouds block the sun from our view.
It's a cloudy day.
What makes the clouds?

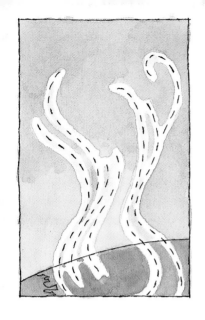 

The sun's heat travels through space.
It warms the earth's oceans, rivers,
    and lakes.
Some of the water evaporates.
It becomes a gas called water vapor.
The water vapor goes up into the air.
It's there—even though you can't see it.

High up, the air is cold.
The water vapor cools.
It changes into tiny drops of water.
They form the clouds in the sky.

You can form a cloud at home.
Ask an adult to boil a pot of water.
The heat evaporates some of the water.
It changes the water into water vapor.
The hot water vapor hits the cool air.
The vapor changes into tiny drops of
	water.
They form a cloud over the pot.

Clouds in the sky have different shapes.

White, fluffy clouds are called
cumulus (KEW-mew-lus).

High, wispy clouds are called
cirrus (SERE-us).

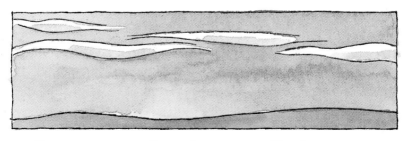

Low, gray clouds are called *stratus*
(STRAT-us).

On cloudy days, the sun is still shining.
But we cannot see the sun.
People in airplanes often fly above the
    clouds.
They can see the sun.

On cloudy days, less sunlight reaches
    earth.
We do not see shadows.
Also, less heat from the sun reaches
    earth.

How's the weather?
Look at the sky.

Rain is falling.
It is coming from dark gray rain clouds.
The tiny drops of water in the rain
 clouds join together.
They grow big and heavy.
They fall as raindrops.

You can make raindrops at home.
Ask an adult to boil a pot of water.
Then hand the adult a pot lid.
Ask the adult to hold the lid in the
cloud over the pot.
Watch little drops of water form under
the pot lid.
Soon they get very big.
Then they fall as raindrops!

Sometimes big rain clouds get a charge
    of electricity.
The electricity sends out a bolt of
    lightning.
The lightning flashes between the
    cloud and earth.
A roar of thunder fills the air.

What should you do during a lightning
   storm?
If outdoors, lie down on the ground.
Stay away from trees or lakes.
If indoors, stay away from open
   windows.
Don't use the telephone or television.

Sometimes drops of rain water freeze
   in the clouds.
They fall as snowflakes.

Go outdoors the next time it snows.
Bring along a dark piece of paper.
Catch some snowflakes on the paper.
Look closely.
All the snowflakes have six sides.
Yet no two are exactly the same!

Sometimes raindrops fall through very
cold air.
They freeze into bits of ice.
We call that sleet.

Sometimes the bits of ice get tossed
about.
Winds blow them up and down inside
the cloud.
More and more water freezes on the ice.
Finally the bigger balls of ice fall.
We call that hail.

How's the weather?
Look at the sky.

The wind is blowing.
Clouds are drifting.
Treetops are swaying.
What makes the wind?

You know that the sun warms the earth.
But some places get warmer than other
places.
Warm air rises.
Cooler air moves in to take its place.
Moving air makes the wind.

You can make a wind too.
Take a warm shower on a cool day.
Watch the shower curtain as you turn
    on the water.
The curtain blows toward the water.
Can you guess why?

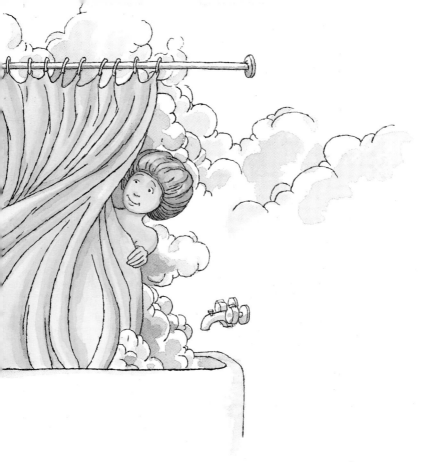

The hot water warms the air in the
    shower.
The warm air rises.
The air in the rest of the bathroom is
    cool.
The cool air rushes into the empty space.
This makes a wind.
It blows the shower curtain.

Air moves at different speeds.

When there is no wind, we say it is calm.

People call a gentle wind a breeze.

A breeze moves at about 10 miles an
hour.

We call a strong wind a gale.

Gale winds blow at about 40 miles an
hour.

Hurricanes are storms with very strong winds.

They strike mostly in warm parts of the world.

Hurricanes usually occur between May and October.

The winds start over the ocean.

They grow stronger and stronger.

The winds may reach up to 150 miles an hour.

That's as fast as a speeding race car!

Tornadoes have the strongest winds.
They mostly occur in the midwestern
  United States.
Tornadoes often start on hot, sticky
  afternoons.
Suddenly a funnel forms beneath a
  heavy, black cloud.
Violent twisting winds sweep across
  the earth.

They can spin around at 200 miles an
 hour.
That's as fast as a plane!

Hurricanes and tornadoes smash
 buildings.
They knock over large trees.
They wreck cars and big trucks.

Look at the sky.
Is it sunny, cloudy, rainy, or windy?
That's the weather today.
But what about the weather tomorrow?
The clues are all around you.
They help you know what the weather
   will be.

Is today's sunset bright and red?
Few clouds at sunset usually mean
   more fair weather.
It will most likely be sunny tomorrow.

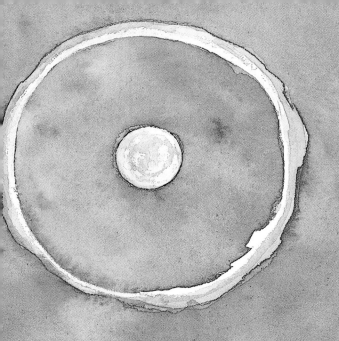

Is there a ring around the moon tonight?
Clouds may be gathering.
This usually means bad weather is
    coming.
It will most likely be stormy or rainy
    tomorrow.

Is the sky clear and the wind light tonight?
This usually means there will be a drop in the temperature.
It will most likely be cooler tomorrow.

Are there lots of clouds tonight?
A cloudy sky usually means a rise in
    temperature.
The weather will most likely be
    warmer tomorrow.

31

Meteorologists are scientists who study
the weather.

They measure conditions

—on the ground

—high above the earth.

They gather information from all over
the globe.

And they put the facts and figures into
huge computers.

Meteorologists then forecast the
    weather.
And they prepare weather maps.
You can hear their forecasts on the
    radio or television.
You can find their weather maps in the
    newspaper or on television.

Many weather forecasts are correct.
But sometimes they are wrong.
Winds and clouds keep moving.
Weather conditions keep changing.
This can make the forecast wrong.

You can use a weather map to forecast
the weather.
Weather maps show big blocks of air.
These blocks of air move over the earth.
This map shows where the air is moving.

Weather often stays the same for
several days.
The blocks of air move slowly or not
at all.
Then they move away.
As they move, the weather changes.

Look at this weather map.

A block of cold air is pushing against a block of warm air.

The place where they meet is called a cold front.

On the map, it is a blue line with points sticking out.

The points show the direction the cold air is moving.

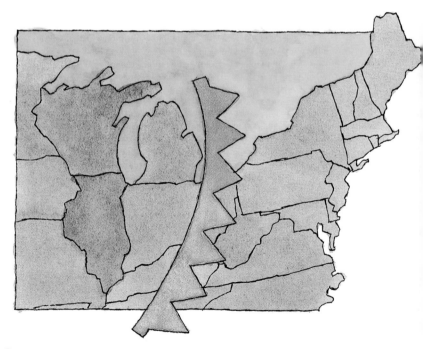

Cold fronts move quickly.
They push the warm air up and out of
the way.
Suddenly strong winds blow.
The weather turns stormy.
Rain or snow may fall.
Thunder and lightning may come too.

Soon the cold front passes.
The sky clears.
The weather gets colder and drier.

Here is another weather map.

A block of warm air is pushing against a block of cold air.

The place where they meet is called a warm front.

On the map, it is a red line with little bumps.

The bumps show the direction the warm air is moving.

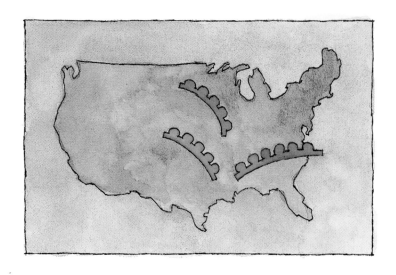

Warm fronts move slowly.
They slide over the cold air.
The winds blow gently along a warm
    front.
Light rain may fall for a few days.

Gradually the warm front passes.
The sky clears.
The weather gets sunny and warmer.

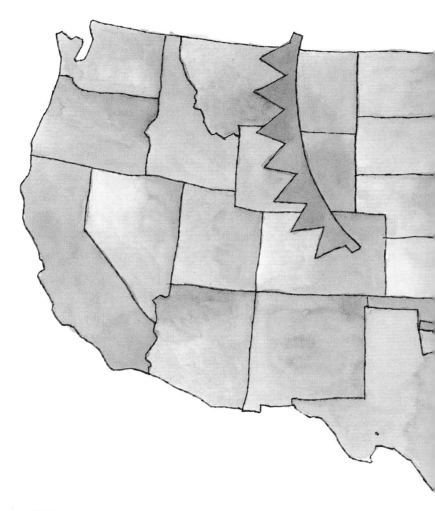

Here is another weather map.
Find the state where you live.
Is a cold front moving toward your
    state?

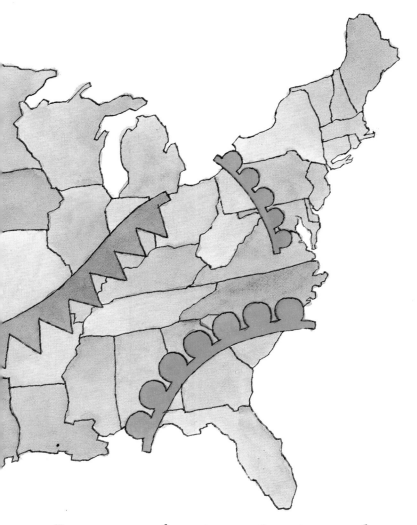

Is a warm front moving toward
   your state?
From this map, what do you think
   your weather will be?

Weather maps sometimes show air
    pressure.
Air pressure is the weight of the air on
    the earth.
You cannot feel the air pressing down.
But it is always there.
And it is always changing.

Sometimes the air pressure is low.
Air rises into the sky.
The air has water vapor.
Clouds form.
The clouds get bigger and darker.
Soon it will rain or snow.

Sometimes the pressure is high.
More air sinks to the ground.
The sky is mostly clear.
Puffy cumulus clouds may appear.
But it will not rain.
The weather will stay dry and sunny.

45

How's the weather?
Look at the sky.

What will the weather be?
Look at the sky—and look at a
weather map!

Index

Property of:
Edison Kenwood Charter School